A TIME TRAVELER'S
JOURNAL
BY NASA

Scripture quotations marked KJV are from the Holy Bible, King James Version (Authorized Version). First published in 1611. Quoted from the KJV Classic Reference Bible, Copyright © 1983 by The Zondervan Corporation.

AuthorHouse™
1663 Liberty Drive
Bloomington, IN 47403
www.authorhouse.com
Phone: 833-262-8899

This book is printed on acid-free paper.

ISBN: 978-1-6655-1153-7 (sc)
ISBN: 978-1-6655-1169-8 (e)

Print information available on the last page.

Published by AuthorHouse 02/25/2021

authorHOUSE

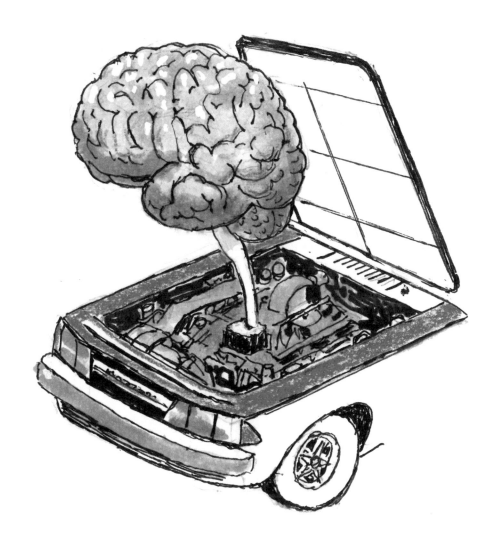

DEDICATION

This is dedicated to my daughter, "My Baby Love"!

Sweetheart, whatever you put your mind to you can do, always know Daddy is behind you.

To Human Beings who want a better future for Humanity and Earth!

ACKNOWLEDGMENTS

Thank you God for giving me life. Thank you for the life you chose for me and I'm praying my good decisions and deeds outweigh my bad ones!

To My Mother, I don't have enough anything that could match what you mean to me… thank you and I love you!

To My Brothers and Family, thank you for listening and the feedback!

Thank you to Rich Richardson, the "World Famous Artist" for each illustration. Rich and I spent hours not only about the illustrations but about life…it was a journey to listen to him every time!

Thank you to Marietta Kouns (Color Copy) and her staff, Ken Smith (KMarks) and Kat Travis a.k.a. "My Team". You all gave this project the professionalism it deserved! Can't wait to do it again!

A very special thank you to Ms. S. Woods, My Friend, My Partner who contributed to me as a person. I can't wait to see you in the future; S&S24E&AD!!!

TABLE OF CONTENTS

The Lord's Weapon

Romans 12:2

And be not conformed to this world but be ye transformed by the renewing of your mind,
that ye may prove what is that good and acceptable, and perfect, will of God.

I am a weapon of the Lord.
The Lord wants His weapon strong.
He starts with the mind.
It is filled with the Lord's words,
His strategy, The Lord's combat tactics.
My mind is the Lord's.
I now meditate...
The Lord teaches me to control breathing, my heart rate.
Mentally feeling every muscle.

I am a weapon of the Lord.
The Lord wants His weapon strong.
My mental and physical muscles are The Lord's.
They are conditioned with His endurance, the Lord's longevity, for many battles.
For a minimum of threescore and ten years,
I am a weapon of The Lord.
The Lord wants His weapon strong

Ephesians 6:12

For we wrestle not against flesh and blood, but against principalities, against powers,
against the rulers of the darkness of this world, against spiritual wickedness in high places.
Amen.

N.A.S.A.

A YOUNG POET'S VIRGINITY

I'm an artist and sensitive about my "ish"
Since I started
Expressing myself
In this
Art form
Performing
A piece to someone
Is like a virgin
Touched
For the first time

My hands shake
Every time
Filled with anxiety
Unsure of what I'm doing
So be gentle if I stumble my lines
I'm fragile-n-tender
But please remember
I'm learning and giving
Something sooo good
From Heaven
Sent to you
How you treat me
Is how I will be
In the future with others

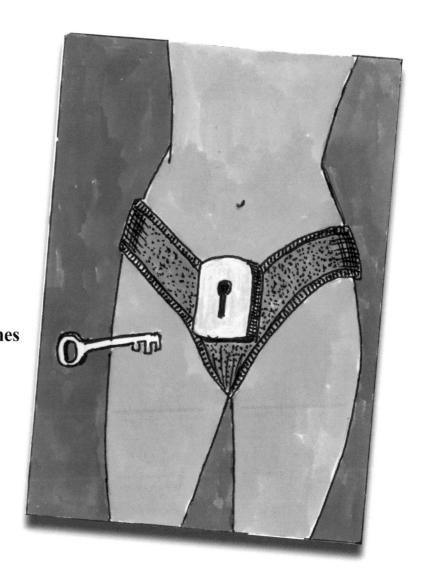

It's my first; it's our first
No safe sex, latex, nor rubbers

Sensual uninhibited
Standing before each other
In our nakedness
Me very, very hesitant
You showing much patience

Anticipating, patiently waiting
The lock; unlocking our virginity
Unleashing us, unchasten us
Painful strokes lead to
Pleasurable rhythms
Taking us to destinations
We have already
Entered
We smell each other's pheromones
Making eye to eye contact
Mouthing, at the same time
With trembling voices
What, is going on?
Verbal virgin Orgasm
Is like I take on this challenge

As my body quakes and quivers
Coming to the ring
In this corner
The number one
Contender

And I told the Lord if he
Allow me to tell my stories
I would attack lines and tracks
With the power he bestowed upon me
To control on earth
Mammals, camels, fish, fowls and
everything

Like His personal warrior
Using my tongue as a double edged
swordsman
A Male lion devouring
Any wilder beast trying
To bring harm to my pride
Promoted head of household by God
Genesis 2:21
One rib He required of me

SOONER OR LATER

I'm 38 now
My birthday I'll be 39
2 houses 2 acres
Like I got 2 life lines
I'm an activist about my grind
Going down my check list (knock, knock)
At the door of "The White House"
Demanding my other 38 acres
With penalties-n-interest
Let's call it 39

First person in line
Mr. President
Reparations
Please send this way
We've been promised this for so long
I done forgot the date
Back when Abraham Lincoln
Had freed the slaves
Written in The Emancipation Proclamay

Blacks still behind because of lack of currency
Currently in the U.S.A.
Foreigners get more reparations
And it's done right in our black faces
It's been done by past and current administrations
So that takes care of sooner and later

Blacks are at a restaurant with the worst waiter
And stereotypically speaking
So you know what I mean
You know how we act about our watermelon, chicken,
And collard greens

Palming something small with a big flash
Blow you outcha mind
Don't worry boutcha body (remember the acres)
I got plenty room and plenty lime
That was to the security guard
I moved to the teller line

Told the teller
Time is money
I'm here to clock mine
Wrist a Samsung Watch
Hand a Glock Nine
If you don't have it now
Ain't no mo later

ODE TO JAZZ

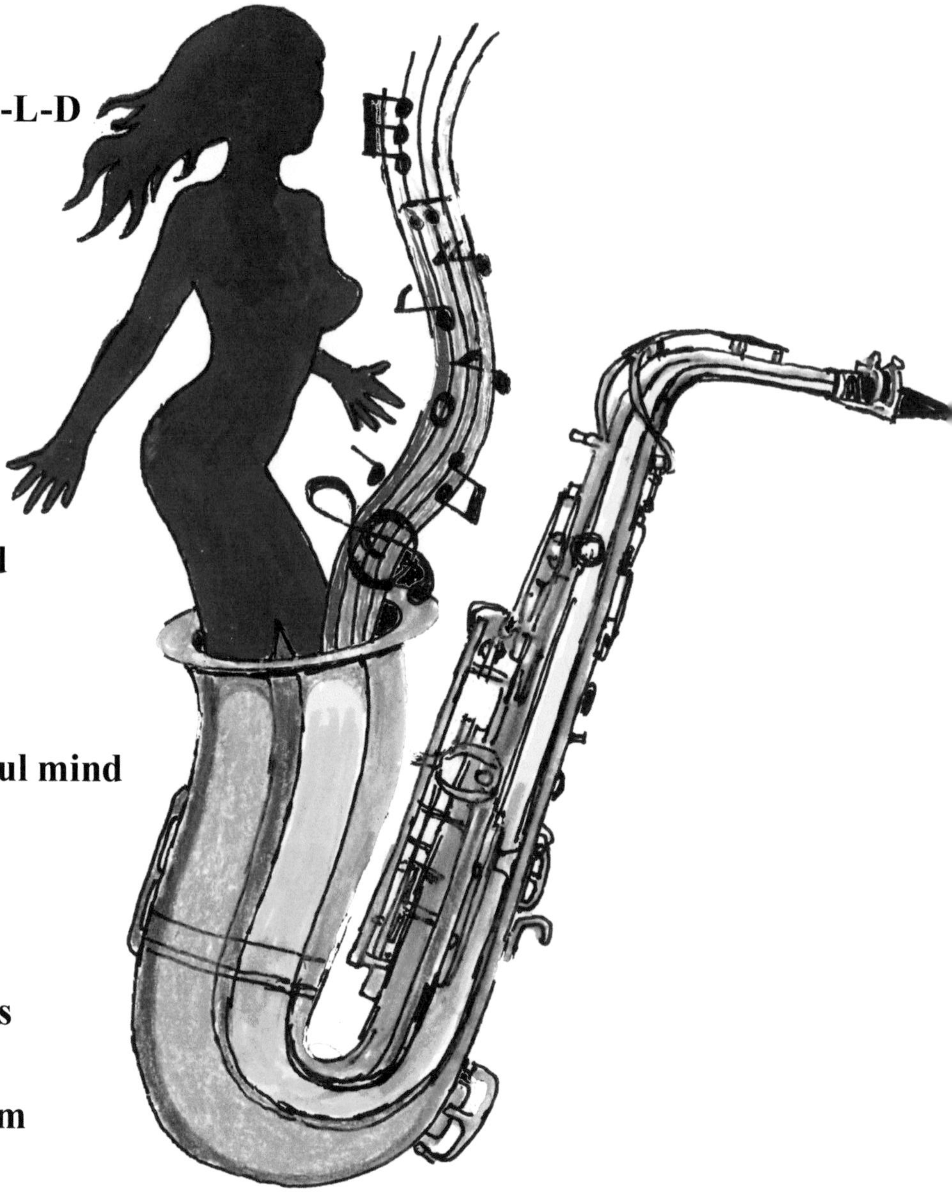

I want my
Metaphors to be as C-O-L-D
As my
Temperature would be
Arms F-O-L-D
Body
In the earth
Six…feet…deep

If you
Took the letters I spelled
To a spelling bee
What you heard
You'll be able to see
Inside a sniper's beautiful mind
Two kill shots
Suspect
One rhyme

Ingesting your eardrums
With a
Flying five finger one arm
Eight pole
Shaolin
Exploding death touch blood on my tongue flow
From severing systems of audio

The world is yours
Right now you're visiting mine
Kick up your feet sit back unwind
Imma continue verbal penetrations
With a
Sexual exploration of
Female and male homo sapiens

Produce female "aah's" and "ooh's"
With hands caressing curves and
grooves
Unlocking sexual combinations
Opening punaani vaults no
complications
Clitorial larcenist
A.K.A cat burglar prowling
Leave it purring after hearing the
kitty meowing

A well placed tongue is very climatic
Let her catch her breath
Then get back at it
Round and round the major, minor
labia
Two fingers stimulate G-spot
Don't play with her
Toes gone curl her voice gone shrill
Withhold breathing
Keep dining on sugar wall meal

2, 1, Lap rocket goes
Smile on her face she already knows
Inside of her
Third alarm fire
Deep V Pearl Diver
Firefighter's Fudge sickle
To tickle her
Sensual
Wet, hot, spot

ROMEO & JULIETTE-FALLING IN LOVE

7 years ago is when I metcha
We lost touch
4 years later
We reconnected

Our Hearts' bonded together
Our Souls' combined
And our Loves' connected

You as the girl of my dreams
From my cerebral cortex
Hand delivered to me
And uss together forever
I imagined
And how now
It seems to have happened

A shower with outcha
Is a quick one or
Alone in there
Is my practice session
Hot water intensing
Pain is Love
Training my skin to endure
So we can have
Hot water fun in the next one

I let her shave
My Mancave
She lets me trim
Her Kitty with clippers
She's my Venus
And I'm her Big Dipper

Crazy and Love
Both have the same brain pattern
Physically on Earth
Making Love mentally and sexually
As cosmic as Saturn

ROMEO & JULIETTE-BEING IN LOVE

I'm in Love with you Too Deep
And you know it
I know it too
By the things my thoughts
Ponder on
When I'm not with you
Your actions are different when you
are far
Verses when you are near
I can't get one response when you're
away
But I get all day and middle of the night
Phone calls, text messages, emojis,
songs-n-videos
When you are here

I'm in Love with you Too Deep
And you know it
I know it too
Because you give me can't sleep
Won't eat, sickening, heart aching pain
Pain that would answer
Why would a dove cry?

What do the tears verify?
Why cry a dove?
It witnessed My Heart's agony
It's tears expressed sadness, mercy
And verified my pain as Love

I'm in Love with you Too Deep
And you know it
I know it too

This burning thing called Love
That fiery ring
Keeps you warm at night
Radiantly satisfying all your needs
thing
Innocently
Love renders ignorance to the brain
Mesmerizing it
With enchanting eyes of dancing flames
While sparking new blazes of desire
Unaware of the intelligence of the fire
Falling prey to its consumption
Entrapped…
With no place to go
This cozy Love Fire
Evolved into a Raging Inferno

I'm in Love with You Too Deep

ROMEO & JULIETTE-TRUE LOVE

I'm sitting in a room all by myself
Yelling for Help
Getting madder and madder
With everyone who said they loved me
Because they haven't responded to my
pleas for help

These pleas have replaced the old me
Slowly, efficiently…effectively
Now what they see
Is a version of me
That is crying for help in different ways

It's been like this for some time
I've had a conversation with each of
them before
Well…kind of
See, in the room
I was talking calmly but not acting
myself
Subtle changes;

Have you been eating?
No just not working out
Easily dismissed
But physical pleas for help
You over here going off again
I'll holla at you later
Nooo, waaait!
I'm just yelling for Help!

I was shutting down and going into
isolation
Or I so lonely
I so long for to be loved
To be Truly Loved!

Only to realize we should have kept it
as lust
Cause when we called it Love
We began its eviction from our Hearts
And Love don't live here anymore
And if I heard you correctly
You just said you were leaving me
today

So if we said we would be together
For forever and a day
Then this is the day after
The day following forever
So that means I have fulfilled my
sentence of Love
To the Death Chamber
Love & Crazy are the same
Have the same brain pattern
Matter can not be destroyed
It will only change forms
And with your words
You have at the same time
Enlightened and darkened My Heart
That to you

It's beating no longer matters
With your words of you leaving me
Have brought death to the particles of
Love
And birth molecules of insanity
In my Heart Matter

See, the heart is a sodium and potassium
pump
To put it plainly
You have caused a chemical imbalance
In the organ that pumps the blood
Carrying vital messages through
vessels
Controlling my body functions
In the medulla oblongata cerebellum

To put it computerally and medically
You have given me a virus that is now
reprogramming me
To no longer act lovingly
But to act Insane slash
Crazy
So my loving hands that use to caress
your neck
Are the same hands that will take your
last breath
And while looking you in your teary
eyes
With tears coming out of mine
Kissing you on the lips
And telling you at the same time

Our souls will be together soon
Cause after ending your life
A bullet will end mine

The smile on your face as you take
your last breath
And the feel of your warm lips
From our last kiss
Gives me the strength to do it
Before your body can turn cold
Blaw!

TIME MACHINE

Have you ever thought about the past and the future
New and old cars, spaceships, and super computers
Like OutKast said, "Back in da days when we were slaves
I bet we was some cool ass people."
Yeah…
How did we get to be hot heads
Solving problems by pulling a trigger
Separated from the knowledge of our own people and
Heritage
Is that what did it?
Not knowing of being Kings and Queens well respected
Or is it the fear from images of your eyes being taken
For looking at a white lady
Are we rebelling for those that
Didn't fight back
When that Birmingham Church went "BOOM"
Are we the ones that for every black man lynched from a
Tree

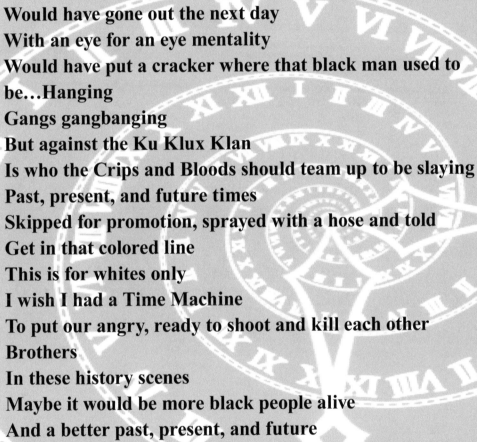

Would have gone out the next day
With an eye for an eye mentality
Would have put a cracker where that black man used to
be...Hanging
Gangs gangbanging
But against the Ku Klux Klan
Is who the Crips and Bloods should team up to be slaying
Past, present, and future times
Skipped for promotion, sprayed with a hose and told
Get in that colored line
This is for whites only
I wish I had a Time Machine
To put our angry, ready to shoot and kill each other
Brothers
In these history scenes
Maybe it would be more black people alive
And a better past, present, and future

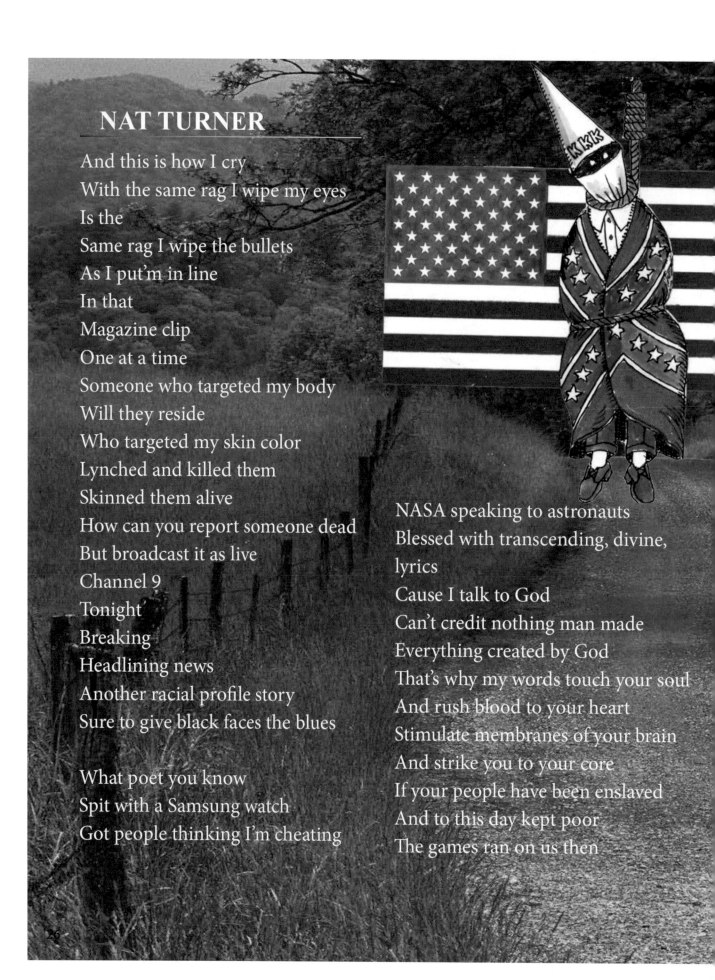

NAT TURNER

And this is how I cry
With the same rag I wipe my eyes
Is the
Same rag I wipe the bullets
As I put'm in line
In that
Magazine clip
One at a time
Someone who targeted my body
Will they reside
Who targeted my skin color
Lynched and killed them
Skinned them alive
How can you report someone dead
But broadcast it as live
Channel 9
Tonight
Breaking
Headlining news
Another racial profile story
Sure to give black faces the blues

What poet you know
Spit with a Samsung watch
Got people thinking I'm cheating

NASA speaking to astronauts
Blessed with transcending, divine,
lyrics
Cause I talk to God
Can't credit nothing man made
Everything created by God
That's why my words touch your soul
And rush blood to your heart
Stimulate membranes of your brain
And strike you to your core
If your people have been enslaved
And to this day kept poor
The games ran on us then

26

Still knock, knock at our door
And we bring our problems
To the same systems that robbed us
before
Federal Government Systems
Ran by J. Edgar Hoover

Who targeted, falsely accused, mur-
dered
Excuse me
Assassinated Huey Newton
Medgar Evers, Fred Hampton,
Harry and Harriette Moore
Malcolm X, Martin Luther
Anyone who tried to motivate and
educate
The black youth

If I tell'm to their face that's what I'm
trying to do
Yoda Chamber
Your own eulogy prepared do you?
One more thing checked off
On my list of things to do
I'm trying to ignite a 2021
Black Panther Party
Mixed with old and new ideals

To deal and build
Thru the years we've gotten smarter
Let's again explore this idea of
Segregation
Sit back and smoke your peace pipe
Take consideration
Give us the opportunity to control
Starting with our own plantations
Our own government, crops, money
Our own education
Our own militant minded,
Armed serve and protect
Black lives matter
Organizations

Nat Turner was born enslaved in Southampton, Virginia and was known as a religious man said to have prophetic visions. In 1828, Turner began receiving instructions to "Slay my enemies with their own weapons", through dreams and visions. A sign/vision on August 13, 1831 begot Turner to set August 21, 1831 as the date for a slave rebellion. While still dark on the Sunday morning of August 21, Nat Turner and about 40 slaves with the desire to be free men, began killing over 55 white slave owners and their families. Nat Turner's slave rebellion is the most famous and successful in the history of the United States of America.

MLK'S NIGHTMARE

Dr. Martin Luther King Jr. delivered his historical elocution "I Have a Dream" on August 28, 1963. Few know the existence of a reporting of Dr. King having a very detailed "nightmare" on August 21, seven days before giving that "World Famous Speech". These are the details of that report...

It was all a nightmare
I had envisioned
I had pictured
Concert Halls, stadiums, I envisioned
People coming to see lil' ole me
On this stage in this vision
Security guards and all to mention

In the crowd all kinds of people
You know you made it when "White Folk" coming to see you
Hello to you in the crowd
While I have your undivided attention
Let me mention
Do not have one confederate flag among you
In your purse, pocket, or tattooed upon you
If you do

The duct tape is going to be wrapped around you
All of you

Don't look at the security guards previously mentioned
They're with me paid from an account of my own pension

No disrespect to the Gay Community
But back to the confederate fag crew mentioned
previously
By the Grace of God you will be able to
Go back to your loved ones, church members,
and secret social
Privately impersonating black culture crews
And in a quiet trembling voice you can say

The New Militant Minded Blacks not for play
By the Grace of God I'm here to say
Everything he did clearly state

After the duct tape's wrapped around
Ankles, wrists, and some mouths
He pointed to a taped up man on the ground
He's going to watch me enjoy hers' right now
He said everyone in the crowd would allow
The ending in store before you right now
All your pleas and pleases will not allow
Any change in your weather forecast of black clouds
It's a thunderstorm the thunder made its sound
The lightning struck when your eyes saw the flash
Ears heard click clack Blaw!

I opened my eyes when the flash flood made its sound

It felt so real. My heart was racing, I was covered in
sweat. It was a nightmare! And I knew a dream was
to come

The poem was created and signed
August 23, 1963; NAS

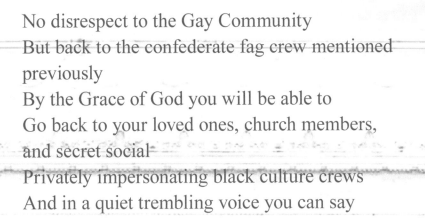

INSANE ASYLUM INTERVIEW

Interviewer: NASA, how did you get put in an Insane Asylum?
NASA: What year is it?
Interviewer: NASA, can you tell me the events that
led to you being taken into custody?
NASA:

I got in the DeLorean with Doc and Marty
Going Back to The Future
Doing cocaine lines with Alexander Graham Bell
Who was on the phone with Benjamin Franklin and
Isaac Newton
After the apple fell
We combined with Einstein
The Third Law of Motion
We came together to define
For every action there is a reaction
The drugs were kickin in
My flexcapacitor was high
Flexcapacitating 88 M-P-Hing
I leaped to the sky

While on my Superman
Flying thru Gotham
Hanging with Batman
While trying to locate the Joker
Smoking Mary Jane before and after
An orgy
With Wonder Woman
And some wonder women
Pretty faces
Painfully grinning
Round, firm, big booties bending
Gobbling, gulping

With no pool
But synchronized swimming
Learned to hold their breath for so long
From Aqua man
Back
When he was pimping

I got on a boat ride
With Popeye
Eating spinach after midnight
With about 10 Gremlins
With no fear
Cause they took the elixir
That turned Mr. Hyde
Back to Dr. Jekyell
And the Hulk
Back to Bruce Banner
Popeye
Was on his way to Smurfville
Cause Bluto-n-Papa Smurf
Got Olive Oil-n-Smurfette
Turning tricks
Addicted to them blue pills
And they ain't cut him in
After the work was put in
Gargamel and Azrael
Were so thankful
We cut a deal with them
And started moving bricks

We went
To the School for the Gifted
Had a sit down with Professor Xavier

And the X-Men
About distribution
Professor X said
Since we've been
Back To The Days of Future Pasts
They controlled everything Northeast
But everything west
Of Sesame Street
Was in the hands of the Boy Wonder
Who teamed up with Agent Smith
And ran the Justice League

They did a Michael Corleone Hit
Took out the 5 families
Of Big Bird,
Elmo, The Count,
Burt and Ernie
Then took all the D-R-U-G's

Xavier said
Since I was an anomaly
He would allow me
To use Cerebro
To contact Neo
Who was on the Nebuchadnezzar
Trippin off red and blue pills
He got from Papa Smurf
And Bluto
Neo said
Travel time would be 30 minutes
But he Wolfed it in 10
Like Marcellus Wallace sent him
And to The Halls of the Justice League
we did go

In the midst of all the fighting-n-shooting
Choke holds, wrastling-n-battling
All the windows and walls
Got to shaking-n-rattling
It was a SWAT Team led by Captain America

He took everyone into custody
And convinced everyone
I was too powerful
For 1 Black Man to be

They would all remain free
If they all blamed me
I would be locked away in an Insane Asylum
Cause no one would believe me
That's what got me here and your visit
But answer 1 question for me…

That happened in 2004, what year is it?

Interviewer: …

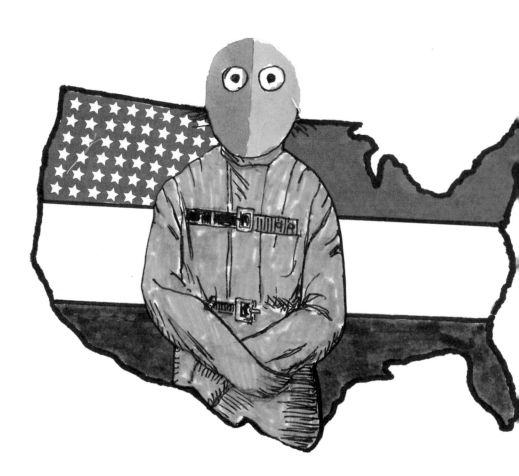

TALKING –ISH LIKE DOLEMITE

I recall a young black man working on
the Titanic
Who kept his head
When the others did panic

I Spring up whenever I Fall back
Carry Summer heat all year thru
Shared some with Ole Man Winter
And turned him back into a youth

I ride hurricanes, typhoons, and
tsunamis
Throughout my life
Been chased by pretty girls, moms, dads,
and whole armies
Daughters trying to get a taste of my
nuts and honey
Parental busy bees banned together
And tried to swarm me
I took out 5 Star Generals
Now I'm the leader of those armies

I broke a mountain top
Bashed a bear, tiger
And a big blue ox
With a lion
I entered a contest of a stare down
Without breaking a sweat or throwing
a blow
He handed over the crown

For 20 hours in the jungle
A lion does sleep

For 20 hours my brain's devouring
Bibles, metaphors, predicates
Nouns, verbs, subjects
Dictionaries, thesauruses-n-all it can eat
So for 4 hours I let the lion reign
And he protects me
During those 4 hours
My brain's still not sleep
Because the Lord is due a tenth of
everything
So for 2.4 hours my eyes are closed
And with God I'm meditating
For the last 1.6
I'm practicing Madden
Trying to be sick on the stick
So at 4 in the morning
I'm already up ain't no yawning
Pen to pad and I'm back to warring
Making my enemies less than before
At war time the death toll includes
Direct hits and friendly fire
Known as casualties of war
It's a verbal fight in the middle of the
street
And nobody was even talking to me
Showing my natural black ass
Opposite of what my momma taught
me to be
At the funeral
Unable to tell which was friend or foe
One thing they gone have in common
Is their casket closed

An unsigned sympathy card attached
with a note
A sum of money for the family
Undisclosed
I'm sending my regrets
Sorry for your loss
Here's an endowment for the family,
expenses, and costs
The money should be equally
proportioned
Black suits for the men to be clean
Black dresses for the women to look
gorgeous
For your loved one's home going
Take my word for it
They knew they had it coming

NASANTHEM

I'm just an
Ole Gangsta talking
Young-n-Cocky
I make a Metaphor float like a Butterfly
And Sting like Ali
I am NASA
Welcome to Time Travel Math Class
A.K.A. 101 Brainatics
By my name Alone
Imma shock the World and cause Havoc

I am a Triple "T" Threat
Thunderstorm to a Tornado
To a Terrorist Attack
Your favorite poet
Scoop'm in the air slam'm cross my knee
Break his back
Run his pockets
Shoes-n-jewels
Semi-Auto to his head
Bbbrrrat

I gave'm the Slightest of Nods
He didn't Acknowledge me Back
So I gave'm a Pai Mei

Happy Ending Body Massage
How Kill Bill is That

Kill any Bill at Will
On paper or Track
My Granddaddy told Me
To a man he did That
It went Quick to gun from Fist
He told me That
He told me This

Don't look for Help
Help Yo'self
Knight Enterprise on the Rise
Now I Appear
Courtesy of M'self

Just an
Ole Gangsta Talking
Young-n-Cocky
I make Metaphors float like a Butterfly
And Sting like Ali
I am NASA
Welcome to Time Travel Math Class
A.K.A. 101 Brainatics
By my name Alone
Imma shock the World and cause Havoc

BRIDGING THE GAP

Life is a journey
Get prepared for the drive then
Know the rules of the road
Before you start driving
Live by God's 10 Commandments
10 Guidelines
Break yo neck before you break
God's 10 Guidelines

Clean your windshield for clear vision
Heed warning signages
Careful who you call friend
The devil, he wear disguises
Friend turn to foe sittin on yo sofa
So surprising
Foe from a distance really friend
You realizing

The Lord and yourself
Is who you should confide in
When peaks turn to valleys
He'll take the wheel
You
Co-pilot then
Get you some Basic Information Before
Leaving Earth
Bible acronym
Hear my Rebel yell
Internally a Rebel crying
In here where you deal with all the
pain
And denialment

Internal cocoon, yeah
Jesus like
Jesus like it when I
Spread my Beautiful Angel Wings
And butterfly it
You would think I was Superman
No on my Last Supper Diet
And if you get a taste
I know you'll like it
I could have started a riot
When that gunman pulled the trigger
On them Christians
And they didn't deny him
Let me calm down
I'm in church
Prayers to the families
From my family
We know it hurt
But want He use'm
He turned that plan around
Totally confused'm
All colors of Christians came together
to rebuke'm
Let me calm down
Church say Amen
Say Amen again
Again and again!

(1) Bridging the Gap- Passing on important knowledge of instilling the foundation in your child, a child, or any human being; whatever place they are in on their journey of life to understand "The Tombstone Dash xxxx-xxxx." Situations are going to occur in your life and you will have to account for the way you deal with them. Bridging the gap between prior to being here (born) to leaving here (death).

(2) Bridging the Gap- Educating the youth properly **on** how things began to where they are now. Including the struggles, bloodshed, and corruption of this country that is not being taught to them.

This piece is also dedicated to the remembrance of the nine victims and three survivors of the Hate Crime on June 17, 2015 at The Emanuel African Methodist Episcopal Church in Charleston, South Carolina.